isolated travels

Hope Irons

BookLeaf
Publishing

India | USA | UK

Presentation by *BookLeaf Publishing*

Web: www.bookleafpub.com

E-mail: info@bookleafpub.com

ISBN: 978-93-5744-978-6

First edition 2022

DEDICATION

To my Jesus, for loving me always and blessing me constantly

PREFACE

I have never claimed to be a writer with any skill, and I probably never will. This short "poetry" collection is merely an expression of my travels, both literally as well as those through my mind, over the past several years. In 2017, on a trip to Central Australia, I felt a surge of creativity in the beautiful environments we were travelling through. Over the course of sixteen days, I wrote many things. I found myself reflecting on me, my mind, my relationships, my desires for my future, and just the general beauty of God's creation. I have never felt like that again, but one day I hope to. This collection is a compilation of those writings, as well as ones written more recently and throughout Melbourne's lockdowns. They portray heartbreak, longing, beauty, pure wonderment, and self-reflection. A lot of them are pretty depressing, or inviting a darker theme. That's not me saying anything about my mental state. For some reason, I'm more inspired in my dark moments than my joyous ones. I guess that's my way of processing my thoughts. A lot of them are pretty cringe and feel like the thoughts of a 12 year old. It should be embarrassing to me that they are, indeed, not.

And I slightly am and also am not. Ultimately, this tiny, tiny book is just a window into random aspects of my life and thoughts. Sometimes it may not make a lot of sense, and other times it definitely will not make sense. If you're confused while reading, there is a 95% chance that that was my intention.
Welcome to the mind of an overthinking teenager/young adult. Thank you for joining me on this adventure.

Moment

I clasp my hands around it,
tight,
not wanting to let go.
I peep through my fingers.
So special,
oh so precious.
I don't know what I'd do if I let it go.

Would it fly away,
wanting someone else to experience it?
Or would it come back?
Like destiny,
having to be with me.

I'm not going to take that chance.
I'm keeping it close,
immersing myself in it,
treasuring it
forever.

After all,
who would want to lose a moment like this?

Unnecessarily Ruined

Clutter
serves no purpose.
It does nothing useful.
It fills empty spaces,
tangible and not.

On a canvas of serenity and tranquillity
we ruin it with
clutter.
It exists to destroy the calm.
Headspace is no longer existent,
already a rare commodity,
and I don't know where to put my foot next.

The mind is a complex expanse,
most remaining unexplored.
So why add more in which to swerve around,
when there is enough distance to be covered
without
the clutter?

Our everyday lives are permeated with mess.

But we feel the need to exacerbate it.
Why add more to think about and act upon,
when there is enough of that to do already
without
the clutter?

Lack of Me

Faith flutters further
and further
away.
I scramble,
grasping
as my past and everything I know
soars
beyond my sight.
I stop
and catch my breath.
But what is left to breathe
without all that has just
escaped me?

Comfortable

I feel like I've been living in a Tupperware
container.
Stuff was piling on top of me,
but eventually someone helped get rid of it,
or it simply rotted and went away.
But not without leaving residue,
marking its place and influence.
I've been comfortable.
I knew everything there was to know
about that container.

Every so often,
the container was washed.
But I hung on,
not wanting to leave
what was comfortable.

This time
when the container has been washed,
I've
let
go.
I'm seeing new places,
hearing new sounds,
experiencing new problems

with new people to help.

I've left what was comfortable,
and now
I'm
here.

Enclosed

Enclosed.
Trapped.
Walls surrounding me,
coming closer
and
closer.
I wonder what they contain.
Other than opal,
stories.
A hundred years ago,
people came down here.
They dug this out.
And now I'm here.

I wonder if the walls
fell around them,
destroying lives
and families,
while trying to find something beautiful.

Enclosed.
Trapped.
Walls surrounding me,
coming closer

and
closer.
My eyes start to close
and my mind drifts away,
thinking of those lives,
the stories,
enclosed in these walls.

The Gap

The rocks stretch high on either side,
a wide path between them.
The gap.

Trees surround me,
a magnificent palette of colours.

People scattered around,
but nothing is said.
Not one word is uttered.
The gap has the power to quieten.
Something so tall and textured
as a rock
can summon

silence.

Divine Routine

"Praise the Lord",
I've been singing since birth
and as I will continue to
all the days of my life.

My blessings,
I owe to Him
despite earning nothing.

His goodness
pervades the earth
even when unacknowledged.

My sinfulness
is not justified,
so I will forever repent.

His forgiveness
is constant
and nothing I ever do will change that.

With a character beyond comprehension,
His love is endless.
So, for all my numbered days,
I will praise Him.

My Zephaniah Prayer

O Lord, teach me to seek and inquire of you.
Teach me to honour you, to do good, and to fill
my house with love and grace.
Teach me not to doubt.

O Lord, help me to seek righteousness and
humility.
Help me to glorify you through everything I do.
Help me to bow before you, with the mountains
and the oceans.

O Lord, show me my place in your kingdom.
Show me how to trust and draw ever nearer to
you.
Show me your goodness in every day.

O Lord, let me wait for you.
Let me witness your passion in every decision
and action.
Let me lie down in your glorious pastures.

O Lord, thank you for your blessings.
Thank you for your power amongst your people.
Thank you for your constant provision and
restoration.
Thank you for your promises to bring us home,
forever.

Not Mine to Understand

I untied the knot.
I let go of the string
that seemed to be holding everything in.
And because
I undid it all,
nothing is the same.

We're two different people
from the same world,
created by the same master
and loved by the same heart.
But,
is that ever going to be enough?

The string ravels away,
just out of my reach.
And if I lean just a bit further,
I can touch the very end.

But I can't grab hold of it.
Not yet anyway.

It may be my story to tell,
but not right now.

As the string slips from sight,
I breathe deeply.

Letting go of control
is all I can do.

Sweet, Blissful Naivety

I try to cry, because my tear ducts ache
from their many dry days,
but I can't.
It's all building up.
And one day, I'm either going to explode
or implode.
Either way,
I don't think I'll survive it.

Please remember me.
Consider that I feel things too.
And ripping it off like a band aid,
like you did,
ripped my heart out along with it.
It showed me very quickly
just how much you still care for me.
Not a single bit.
Which is good for you, I guess.
But for me.
That's another story.

One day, I'll look back fondly

on the many hours we spent together
in sweet, blissful naivety,
but that'll be it.
I'll be happy with someone,
and so will you.
I look forward to that day,
for the both of us.

Stupid Puppy Love

Will I be forever
letting go?

He said I was his
everything.

'Always and forever,
until the day I die.'

All innocent lies.

You didn't fight for me
but I need someone who will.

From everything to nothing,
just like that.

I won't make a mistake like you
ever again.

How damn naïve.

Debris Causing

Jealousy enrages within me,
tearing a crooked path through my anatomy.
It's unpredictable.
It disturbs the heart from truly loving,
distracts the lungs from regular breath,
causes the feet to stumble while they were just
minding their own business.

But it will not go away.
No matter how hard I beg,
it is stronger than I ever was.
So, I sit and suffer
in a constant state of conflict,
watching life unfold around me whilst
jealousy enrages within me.

Loss

One day I long to look up at the stars and see
you,
who I miss so.
As my heart aches for your embrace,
my arms limp at my side, purposeless,
as my mind struggles to comprehend,
my legs failing in keeping me upright,
I know I must go on.

I pray the stars show me something
beyond my human comprehension,
something supernatural and fantastical.
It is only that which can stitch together
the strings torn from my heart,
which refuse to heal without your love.

Oh God, send me a sign.
May Jupiter be obvious to the plain eyes,
so I may spin under the night sky and be graced
by a galactic embrace.
How do I go on when a life,
so precious,
has been stolen too early?

Until I have an answer,

I will long to look up at the stars and see you.
I want to see you in planets,
constellations,
moons,
asteroids.
They are all out of my reach,
just like you.
But for the time being,
at least I can reminisce and stand in absolute
awe of everything above.

Day 254

Loneliness or isolation.
The great divide.
One, so deliberate and the other,
not.
Permanent or temporary.
It's hard to tell in the moment.
Things change day to day
and yet,
nothing changes.
The lack of change,
and subsequent loneliness,
proves permanent
but it's only because we're in
'unprecedented' times.
Thus,
it's temporary.
Temporary isolation,
yet
seemingly endless loneliness.
Temporary loneliness,
yet
isolation that stretches over years.
The indistinguishable
(and not-so-great)
divide.

Nothing Ever Changes

Sometimes you have to convince yourself
you can get through a day
or a week
or a month
or a year.
Or two.
When the days drag into each other,
indistinguishable from one another
because nothing ever changes,
you're hanging off the edge of your seat
to see if something will change.
But nothing does.

But,
when it does,
when the rare occurrence of variety comes to be
it is inevitability fleeting.
Here for a moment,
and gone for a longer one.
It's been like that for two years.
The only predictability
is that nothing ever changes.

We now raise our kids with an innate sense of
pessimism.
Everything must come with a grain of salt.

Everyday looks the same,
but even when it doesn't,
we don't expect it to last,
even when we're told that it will.
'Trust us'.
No.
This is what we do now,
and it is how we must operate.
In a world where nothing ever changes,
your heart hardens to hope.
It's a survival mechanism.
A day-to-day essential.

We must convince ourselves to endure
each day,
each week,
each month,
each year.
Or two.
While some people thrive,
others are merely surviving
in this period where nothing ever changes.
Soon it will be over.
Soon it must be over.
But who's to say for sure?

Angsty, Juvenile (so far from poetic) Rant

Have you ever noticed how society has normalised
so many things that just shouldn't be?
Mental illness:
everyone's got it.
Poverty:
damn, better get around to doing something
about that.
Christianity:
considered absolutely unacceptable and
outdated.
Soaring prices in a generation that is paid less
and less:
they're just not working hard enough.
Burnout:
good, it means you're busy, so keep it up.
Environmental degradation:
it's all big companies' faults and I can do
nothing.

Today's young adults are suffering because there
is an
undeniable, suffocating pressure to live up to
our grandparents' standards in a world that
moved on a long time ago.
They created their world,
and we need to be left to create our own.
Instead, we're given these standards to meet.
Standards that dictate our livelihoods,
faith,
social status,
careers and work ethic.
I could go on.
Young people are outraged at politicians for
doing nothing,
yet older people get angry that they 'do nothing'.

But we're trying to do something.
We're just not allowed.
We're told the world is a fine place to live.
Accept how it is and move on.
If you want to see change, make it happen,
but there's no point.
It's this new generation and all their mental
issues,
that's what is causing today's tensions.
It couldn't be outdated policies,
expectations,
environments,

people.
I could go on.
In a world that needs to change so we can live,
we're told we're just anxious and stressed over
nothing.

Yet that stress is praised because it means we're
working hard.
Apparently for the wrong causes though.
To please the ones we don't want to,
we'd have to accept the world the way it is
and not fight for peace, justice, equity.
I could go on.
We become tired of 'going on',
but we don't give ourselves a choice because the
alternative is desired by no one.
The normalisation of the destruction of the
environment,
of the destruction of people if they believe the
wrong things,
of the destruction of people's wellbeing if
they're not coping,
of the destruction of people's livelihoods if they
don't live according to the norm.
It's destroying us.
I could go on.

Politics of People

Decisions split our families,
our communities,
our countries,
our world.

Divisive is our world,
a world and people which knows no better.
It's hard to 'know better'
when we are dictated specific ideologies.

These ideologies tear us apart,
but they don't have to.
Ideologies are not people.
People care where beliefs don't.

Caring about the people
despite choices, innate beliefs
and so much more
would surely fix the globe.

You'd hope so anyway.
Otherwise,
what hope do we have for a future
free from deadly divisiveness?

Meet: Anxiety

She's a young woman
filled with Anxiety.
She has a Faith that sometimes wavers.
She loves people
but they scare her.
She has a desire to see good done.

But it's never that easy.
Anxiety rises
and takes over.
Out of her control, Anxiety consumes all.
It feels unstoppable.
She doesn't know what to do.

Anxiety ripples, never consistent.
Anxiety comes and goes,
shocking and disrupting,
a lack of consideration shown by Anxiety.
Anxiety doesn't care for people,
like she does.

Anxiety aims to define people.
She doesn't like it,
but she can't help it.

As Anxiety takes over, she feels herself
disappearing.
Disappearing to the fear,
the fear of permanent worry.

She pastes on a smile
as she wakes up each morning.
She puts on clothes
that won't draw attention.
She goes places
where she can hide from Anxiety.

But Anxiety follows.
It's in their nature.
That doesn't make them blameless.
Anxiety loves to destroy relationships.
The young woman feels the strain,
and it's almost unbearable.

Anxiety loves when people are burdened.
The people hate it.
She is devoured by Anxiety.
Day by day,
she doesn't get a break.
It is becoming unbearable.

Her Faith starts to waver,
which is Anxiety's favourite past-time.
She starts to question

as Anxiety brings in doubt.
As doubt creeps in,
she starts to lose Faith.

When people try to help,
Anxiety pushes them away.
She is filled with guilt,
but Anxiety makes her feel helpless.
The stress continues,
and it is unbearable.

But over time she realises,
Anxiety doesn't have to rule.
Anxiety has no authority.
Anxiety is powerless.
Anxiety is purposeless.

She starts to gain control
as she shoves Anxiety away.
She reclaims her Faith
as she shoves aside her doubt.

Anxiety nearly overcame her,
but Faith and Resilience saved the day.
They saved her.

Anxiety never disappears,
but instead, Faith overcomes.

The young woman will forever be grateful for her Faith.

My Body, The Dictator

The burning in my chest
tells me to take a breath.
The pounding in my head
tells me to think about something else.
The jittering of my legs
tells me to take a walk.
The darting of my eyes
tells me to shut them tight.

It's all well and good thinking these things
but acting on them is another issue.
While my chest pounds
and my head darts,
while my legs burn
and my eyes jitter,
the tension rises and rises
making it impossible to
think
clearly
and
act
accordingly.

I breathe and think of a moment happier than
this one,
while I walk with my eyes shut,
head tilted back to accept the sun's rays.
I feel the tension ooze from the soles of my feet,
into the pavement below.
As the stress scuttles away like ants to their
queen,
my eyes open to the world around once again
so I can simply think clearly and act accordingly.

Proverbs 17:17 and I

In a time of depression,
of darkness,
of loneliness,
of sorrow,
you lent a hand.
You bent down, stooping to meet my eyes
and loved me.
You said 'thank you,
I couldn't have made it without you.'
And without knowing it,
you're the one saving me.

I'll Leave You With This...

Let me leave you with my heart,
the heart that is scratched from my nails
tearing the hurt away.
The heart that is bruised from being passed
around
to too many people.
But, the heart that always loved
with every bit of its capacity.

Let me leave you with my head,
the head that is permanently marked
by every thought.
The head that anxiety tried to destroy
too many times to count.
But, the head that was always level,
fair and just.

Let me leave you with my hands,
the hands that held on when they shouldn't have
and have the scars to prove it.
The hands that cradled yours
even when it wasn't their job.

But, the hands that will continue working
until the day they are too frail to twitch.

Let me leave you with my feet,
the feet that dragged themselves and everyone
else
through every storm.
The feet that are not perfect
because they were trodden on too many times.
But, the feet that are tough
because they persevered.

I'll leave you with these,
all the best pieces of me.
Though they are scratched, bruised, scarred
and permanently marked,
they are stronger because of it.
These pieces of me
are irreplaceable.

I'll leave you with these
because I cannot trust another soul with them.
So, my friend,
please handle them with care.
Until I see you again,
if such a time should come,
you are loved by every piece of me, and you
hold the things that prove it.